ETHICAL AND LEGAL ISSUES IN RESPIRATORY CARE

TABLE OF CONTENTS

INTRODUCTION 2

MODULE ONE 3
    LESSON ONE: ETHICS IN RESPIRATORY CARE 3
    LESSON TWO: LEGAL FOUNDATIONS IN HEALTHCARE 7

MODULE TWO 11
    LESSON ONE: PATIENT RIGHTS AND INFORMED CONSENT 11
    LESSON TWO: CONFIDENTIALITY AND PRIVACY IN RESPIRATORY CARE 15

MODULE THREE 19
    LESSON ONE: ETHICAL DILEMMAS AND DECISION-MAKING IN RESPIRATORY CARE 19
    LESSON TWO: PROFESSIONALISM AND ETHICAL PRACTICE IN RESPIRATORY CARE 22

MODULE FOUR 26
    LESSON ONE: LEGAL RESPONSIBILITIES AND RISK MANAGEMENT IN RESPIRATORY CARE 26

MODULE FIVE 30
    LESSON ONE: PROFESSIONAL DEVELOPMENT AND ADVOCACY IN RESPIRATORY CARE 30

MODULE SIX 33
    LESSON ONE: ETHICAL LEADERSHIP AND PROFESSIONAL RESPONSIBILITY 33

MODULE SEVEN 37
    LESSON ONE: THE FUTURE OF ETHICS AND LEGAL ISSUES IN RESPIRATORY CARE 37

CONCLUSION 40

REFERENCES 41

COURSE OVERVIEW

This course provides an in-depth examination of the ethical and legal issues that respiratory therapists encounter in clinical practice. It is designed to equip healthcare providers with the knowledge and skills necessary to navigate complex ethical dilemmas, adhere to legal standards, and deliver patient-centered care. The course covers a broad range of topics including foundational ethical principles, legal responsibilities, patient rights, informed consent, professionalism, cultural competence, and the impact of technological advancements on respiratory care.

COURSE OBJECTIVES

By the end of this course, participants will be able to Understand and Apply Ethical Principles, Navigate Legal Responsibilities, Protect Patient Rights and Ensure Confidentiality, Enhance Professionalism and Ethical Practice, Develop Cultural Competence and Promote Diversity, Lead and Advocate for the Profession, Prepare for Future Ethical and Legal Challenges and, Promote Professional Development and Advocacy. This comprehensive course overview and the specific objectives aim to provide a clear roadmap for participants, guiding them through the critical aspects of ethics and legal issues in respiratory care and preparing them to handle real-world challenges effectively.

COURSE MATERIALS

To learn this course, **healthcare providers/ participants** must be provided with materials like a Pen, pencil, notebook, and notepad to better understand and make it easy for them to learn.

INTRODUCTION

In the ever-evolving landscape of healthcare, respiratory care practitioners play a critical role in ensuring the well-being of patients with respiratory disorders. The field demands not only a high level of technical expertise but also a deep understanding of ethical and legal principles that guide professional conduct. "Navigating Ethics and Legal Issues in Respiratory Care: A Comprehensive Guide for Healthcare Providers" aims to serve as an essential resource for healthcare providers who are dedicated to delivering ethical, legal, and high-quality care to their patients.

Healthcare providers are frequently confronted with complex situations that require a balance between clinical decision-making, ethical considerations, and legal obligations. Respiratory care, in particular, involves unique challenges due to the critical nature of respiratory functions and the vulnerability of patients who depend on respiratory support. This book addresses these challenges by providing a thorough examination of the ethical and legal issues specific to respiratory care.

Ethics in healthcare is a broad and multifaceted domain that encompasses principles such as autonomy, beneficence, non-maleficence, and justice. These principles are the bedrock of patient-centered care and guide healthcare providers in making decisions that respect the dignity and rights of patients. In respiratory care, ethical considerations often involve end-of-life decisions, the allocation of scarce resources, and the management of chronic illnesses. This book delves into these issues, offering insights and strategies to navigate the ethical complexities that arise in practice.

MODULE ONE

LESSON ONE: ETHICS IN RESPIRATORY CARE

Ethics in healthcare serves as the cornerstone for clinical practice, shaping the interactions between healthcare providers and patients, and guiding decision-making processes. In respiratory care, where patients often face critical health challenges, ethical considerations become particularly significant.

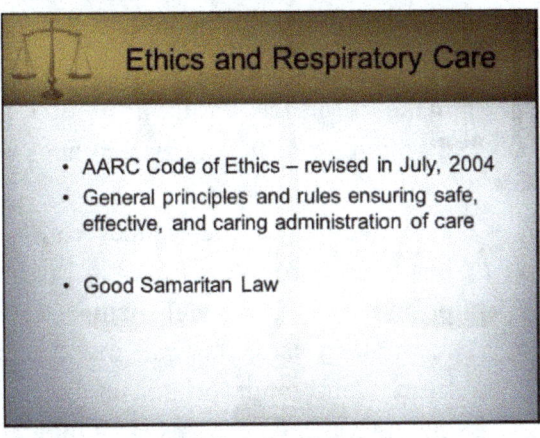

The Importance of Ethics in Respiratory Care

Ethics is essential in respiratory care for several reasons. Firstly, it ensures that patient welfare remains the primary focus of care. Ethical principles such as autonomy, beneficence, non-maleficence, and justice provide a framework that helps healthcare providers make decisions that are in the best interest of their patients. Respiratory therapists often work with vulnerable populations, including the elderly, infants, and critically ill patients, making the need for ethical vigilance even more critical.

Secondly, adherence to ethical standards fosters trust between patients and healthcare providers. Trust is a fundamental component of the therapeutic relationship and is crucial for effective patient care. Patients who trust their healthcare providers are more likely to adhere to treatment plans and engage in open communication, which can significantly impact health outcomes.

Key Ethical Principles in Respiratory Care

- Autonomy: This principle emphasizes the right of patients to make informed decisions about their own healthcare. In respiratory care, respecting patient autonomy involves providing comprehensive information about treatment options, potential outcomes, and risks, enabling patients to make informed choices. It also means honoring advance directives and patient preferences, particularly in end-of-life care.
- Beneficence: Beneficence refers to the obligation of healthcare providers to act in the best interest of the patient, promoting their well-being and preventing harm. In respiratory care, this can involve actions such as providing timely and appropriate interventions, advocating for the patient's needs, and ensuring that care is patient-centered and compassionate.
- Non-maleficence: Closely related to beneficence, non-maleficence means "do no harm." Respiratory therapists must carefully consider the potential risks and benefits of treatments and interventions, striving to minimize harm while maximizing therapeutic benefits. This principle is particularly important in procedures like intubation and mechanical ventilation, where the risks can be significant.
- Justice: The principle of justice relates to fairness and equality in healthcare. It requires that healthcare providers distribute resources and care equitably, without discrimination. In respiratory care, this can involve ensuring that all patients have access to necessary treatments, regardless of their socioeconomic status, race, or other factors. It also includes advocating for fair policies and practices within healthcare institutions and the broader healthcare system.

Ethical Issues in Respiratory Care

Respiratory care practitioners encounter a range of ethical issues in their practice. Some of the most common include:

- End-of-Life Decisions: Respiratory therapists often work with patients who have life-limiting conditions. Making decisions about continuing or withdrawing life-sustaining treatments, such as mechanical ventilation, involves complex ethical considerations. Practitioners must balance the principles of autonomy, beneficence, non-maleficence, and justice while considering the wishes of the patient and their family.
- Allocation of Resources: In times of crisis, such as during a pandemic, respiratory therapists may face situations where resources like ventilators are scarce. Ethical decision-making in these scenarios involves determining how to allocate limited resources fairly and effectively, ensuring that decisions are guided by ethical principles rather than bias or external pressures.
- Informed Consent: Obtaining informed consent is a critical ethical responsibility. Patients must be fully informed about the nature of their condition, the proposed treatments, potential risks, and alternatives. Ensuring that patients understand this information and consent voluntarily is essential for respecting their autonomy.
- Patient Confidentiality: Maintaining patient confidentiality is a fundamental ethical obligation. Respiratory therapists must ensure that patient information is protected and only shared with those who have a legitimate need to know. This is particularly important in an age where electronic health records and data sharing are common.

Strategies for Ethical Decision-Making

To navigate ethical dilemmas effectively, respiratory care practitioners can employ several strategies:

- Ethical Frameworks: Utilizing established ethical frameworks can provide a structured approach to decision-making. Frameworks such as the Four-Box Method, which considers medical indications, patient preferences, quality of life, and contextual features, can help clarify complex situations.

- Ethics Committees: Many healthcare institutions have ethics committees that can provide guidance and support when facing difficult ethical decisions. These committees can offer multidisciplinary perspectives and help ensure that decisions are well-considered and ethically sound.
- Continuous Education: Staying informed about ethical issues and best practices through continuous education and training is crucial. Attending workshops, seminars, and conferences on medical ethics can enhance a practitioner's ability to make ethical decisions.
- Reflective Practice: Engaging in reflective practice allows healthcare providers to critically analyze their experiences and decisions. Reflective practice involves considering the outcomes of past decisions, identifying areas for improvement, and applying these insights to future practice.

Ethics in respiratory care is a vital component of professional practice. By adhering to ethical principles, respiratory therapists can ensure that they provide high-quality, compassionate care that respects the dignity and rights of patients. Understanding and applying these principles in everyday practice helps to build trust, promote patient well-being, and navigate the complex ethical landscapes that healthcare providers frequently encounter.

DISCUSSION QUESTIONS

- How do ethical principles such as autonomy, beneficence, non-maleficence, and justice apply specifically to respiratory care practices?
- Can you think of a scenario in respiratory care where ethical principles might conflict? How would you resolve such a conflict?

LESSON TWO: LEGAL FOUNDATIONS IN HEALTHCARE

The practice of respiratory care, like all healthcare professions, is governed by a complex web of laws, regulations, and standards designed to protect patients and ensure the delivery of safe and effective care. Understanding these legal foundations is essential for respiratory therapists to navigate their professional responsibilities and avoid legal pitfalls. This lesson provides an overview of the key legal concepts and frameworks that underpin healthcare practice.

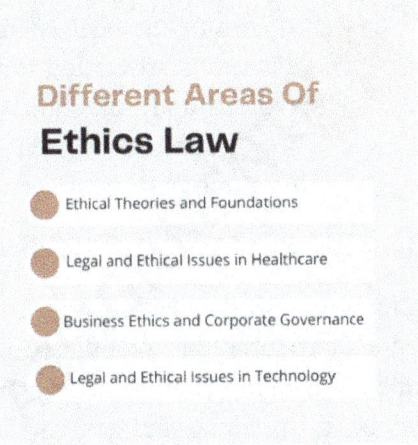

The Legal Framework in Healthcare

The legal framework for healthcare in the United States is comprised of federal and state laws, regulations from government agencies, and standards set by professional organizations. This framework establishes the rules and guidelines that healthcare providers must follow to ensure compliance and protect patient rights.

- Federal Laws and Regulations: Federal laws such as the Health Insurance Portability and Accountability Act (HIPAA) and the Emergency Medical Treatment and Labor Act (EMTALA) set national standards for patient privacy, emergency care, and other aspects of healthcare delivery. Agencies like the Centers for Medicare & Medicaid Services (CMS) and the Food and Drug Administration (FDA) regulate various aspects of healthcare practice and ensure compliance with federal standards.
- State Laws and Regulations: Each state has its own set of laws and regulations that govern the practice of healthcare within

its borders. These laws cover areas such as licensure, scope of practice, and professional conduct. State medical boards and other regulatory bodies oversee the enforcement of these laws and handle disciplinary actions against healthcare providers.
- Professional Standards: Professional organizations such as the American Association for Respiratory Care (AARC) develop standards and guidelines for the practice of respiratory care. These standards often go beyond legal requirements, promoting best practices and high standards of care.

Licensure and Scope of Practice

Licensure is a critical aspect of the legal framework for respiratory care. It ensures that healthcare providers meet specific educational and competency requirements before they are allowed to practice. The scope of practice defines the activities that licensed respiratory therapists are authorized to perform.

- Licensure Requirements: To obtain a license, respiratory therapists must complete an accredited educational program, pass a national certification exam, and meet any additional state-specific requirements. Maintaining licensure typically requires ongoing education and adherence to professional standards.
- Scope of Practice: The scope of practice for respiratory therapists varies by state but generally includes activities such as performing diagnostic tests, administering respiratory treatments, and managing mechanical ventilation. Understanding the scope of practice is crucial to ensure that respiratory therapists do not engage in activities beyond their legal authorization.

Patient Rights and Legal Protections

Patient rights are a fundamental aspect of healthcare law. These rights are designed to protect patients and ensure they receive safe, respectful, and informed care.

- Informed Consent: Informed consent is a legal requirement that ensures patients are fully informed about the risks, benefits, and alternatives of a proposed treatment before agreeing to it. This process involves clear communication between the healthcare provider and the patient, allowing the patient to make an informed decision about their care.
- Confidentiality and Privacy: Protecting patient confidentiality is a legal obligation under laws like HIPAA. Respiratory therapists must ensure that patient information is kept private and only disclosed with the patient's consent or as required by law.
- Right to Refuse Treatment: Patients have the right to refuse treatment, even if it may result in harm or death. Respecting this right involves acknowledging the patient's autonomy and providing information about the potential consequences of refusing treatment.

Legal Responsibilities and Liability

Healthcare providers, including respiratory therapists, have a duty to adhere to the standard of care in their practice. Failure to meet this standard can result in legal liability.

- Standard of Care: The standard of care refers to the level of care that a reasonably competent healthcare provider would provide under similar circumstances. This standard is determined by factors such as professional guidelines, clinical evidence, and expert opinions.
- Negligence and Malpractice: Negligence occurs when a healthcare provider fails to meet the standard of care, resulting in harm to the patient. Malpractice is a specific type of negligence that involves a breach of duty by a licensed professional. To establish malpractice, the plaintiff must prove that the provider owed a duty to the patient, breached that duty, and caused harm as a result.
- Documentation and Record-Keeping: Accurate and thorough documentation is essential for legal protection. Medical

records serve as evidence of the care provided and can be crucial in defending against allegations of negligence or malpractice. Respiratory therapists must ensure that their documentation is clear, complete, and timely.

Risk Management and Legal Compliance

Proactive risk management and compliance with legal requirements are essential for minimizing legal risks and ensuring high-quality care.

- Risk Management Strategies: Implementing risk management strategies such as regular training, adherence to protocols, and continuous quality improvement can help identify and mitigate potential risks. Engaging in open communication and fostering a culture of safety also contribute to reducing errors and improving patient outcomes.
- Legal Compliance: Compliance with laws, regulations, and professional standards is mandatory for all healthcare providers. Staying informed about changes in the legal landscape and participating in ongoing education can help respiratory therapists maintain compliance and avoid legal issues.

Understanding the legal foundations of healthcare is crucial for respiratory therapists to practice safely and effectively. By familiarizing themselves with federal and state laws, professional standards, and ethical principles, healthcare providers can navigate the complexities of their profession with confidence.

DISCUSSION QUESTIONS

- What are some key legal responsibilities of respiratory therapists, and how do they impact daily practice?
- How can respiratory therapists stay informed about changes in laws and regulations that affect their practice?

MODULE TWO

LESSON ONE: PATIENT RIGHTS AND INFORMED CONSENT

Respiratory care like all areas of healthcare, is founded on the principle of patient-centered care. Central to this principle is the recognition and protection of patient rights,

Patient's Rights

- All patients have the right to:
  - Give informed consent
  - Be informed of advantages and potential risks of treatment – informed consent
    - Implied
    - Informed
  - Refuse treatment
  - Privacy (HIPAA)
  - Confidentiality
    - Privileged communication (HIPAA)

as well as the practice of obtaining informed consent. In this lesson, we will delve into the significance of patient rights, the process of obtaining informed consent, and the ethical and legal considerations that accompany these practices.

Understanding Patient Rights

Patient rights encompass a set of ethical and legal principles that safeguard the autonomy, dignity, and well-being of individuals seeking healthcare services. These rights serve as a foundation for the therapeutic relationship between patients and healthcare providers and are essential for upholding trust and mutual respect.

- Autonomy: At the core of patient rights is the principle of autonomy, which grants individuals the freedom to make decisions about their own healthcare. This includes the right to refuse treatment, participate in care decisions, and access information necessary to make informed choices.

- Dignity and Respect: Patients have the right to be treated with dignity and respect at all times. This includes considerations for cultural, religious, and personal beliefs, as well as the protection of privacy and confidentiality.
- Access to Information: Patients have the right to receive clear, accurate, and understandable information about their diagnosis, treatment options, risks, and benefits. Healthcare providers have an obligation to communicate effectively and address any questions or concerns that patients may have.
- Quality of Care: Patients have the right to receive high-quality care that meets established standards and respects their individual needs and preferences. This includes timely access to appropriate treatments and interventions, as well as continuity of care throughout the healthcare journey.

The Importance of Informed Consent

Informed consent is a cornerstone of ethical healthcare practice and is rooted in the principle of respect for patient autonomy. It involves providing patients with comprehensive information about their condition, treatment options, potential risks, and alternatives, allowing them to make voluntary and informed decisions about their care.

- Components of Informed Consent: Informed consent consists of several key components, including disclosure, comprehension, voluntariness, and capacity. Disclosure requires healthcare providers to communicate relevant information to patients in a clear and understandable manner. Comprehension ensures that patients understand the information provided and can make informed decisions based on that knowledge. Voluntariness requires that patients freely consent to or refuse treatment without coercion or undue influence. Capacity refers to the patient's ability to understand the information provided and make decisions based on that understanding.

- Obtaining Informed Consent: The process of obtaining informed consent involves a dialogue between the healthcare provider and the patient, during which information is shared, questions are answered, and decisions are made collaboratively. Healthcare providers must assess the patient's capacity to provide consent and ensure that they have the information necessary to make an informed decision.
- Exceptions to Informed Consent: While informed consent is generally required for medical interventions, there are certain exceptions, such as emergencies, therapeutic privilege, and waiver of consent. In emergencies where immediate treatment is necessary to prevent harm, obtaining formal consent may not be feasible. In such cases, healthcare providers must prioritize the patient's well-being while respecting their autonomy to the extent possible.

Ethical and Legal Considerations

Respecting patient rights and obtaining informed consent are not only ethical imperatives but also legal requirements. Failure to obtain valid informed consent can result in legal liability and compromise the integrity of the therapeutic relationship.

- Legal Standards: Laws and regulations governing informed consent vary by jurisdiction but generally require healthcare providers to disclose relevant information to patients, ensure comprehension, and obtain voluntary consent. Deviations from these standards may constitute negligence or malpractice and could lead to legal consequences.
- Documentation: Documentation of the informed consent process is essential for legal protection and accountability. Healthcare providers should document the discussions with patients, including the information provided, questions asked, and decisions made, as well as any consent forms signed by the patient.
- Shared Decision-Making: Shared decision-making is an approach that involves collaborating with patients to make

healthcare decisions based on their preferences, values, and clinical evidence. This approach enhances patient autonomy and promotes a more patient-centered care experience.

Challenges and Strategies

Despite its importance, obtaining informed consent can present challenges in clinical practice. Language barriers, cognitive impairments, and time constraints are just a few examples of factors that may complicate the consent process. To address these challenges, healthcare providers can employ several strategies:

- Use of Interpreters: Utilizing interpreters or language assistance services can help overcome language barriers and ensure effective communication with patients who speak languages other than English.
- Patient Education Materials: Providing written materials in a patient's preferred language can supplement verbal explanations and reinforce key information about their condition and treatment options.
- Sensitivity to Cultural Differences: Recognizing and respecting cultural differences in healthcare decision-making is essential. Healthcare providers should be mindful of cultural beliefs, practices, and preferences that may influence how patients perceive and approach consent.
- Training and Education: Ongoing training and education for healthcare providers on communication skills, cultural competence, and ethical principles can improve their ability to navigate complex consent discussions and address patient concerns effectively.

DISCUSSION QUESTIONS

- Why is patient confidentiality crucial in respiratory care, and what are the potential consequences of breaches in confidentiality?

- How should a respiratory therapist handle a situation where a patient's right to privacy conflicts with the need to share information for their care?

LESSON TWO: CONFIDENTIALITY AND PRIVACY IN RESPIRATORY CARE

Confidentiality and privacy are fundamental principles in healthcare that protect patient information and promote trust between patients and healthcare providers. In respiratory care, where sensitive medical information is routinely collected and shared, maintaining confidentiality and privacy is essential for upholding ethical standards and legal requirements. This lesson explores the importance of confidentiality and privacy in respiratory care, the ethical considerations involved, and strategies for safeguarding patient information.

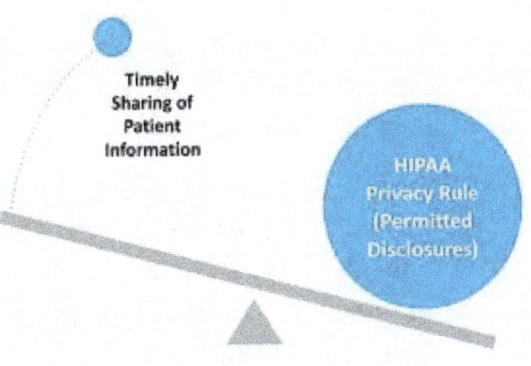

Understanding Confidentiality and Privacy

Confidentiality refers to the obligation of healthcare providers to protect patient information from unauthorized disclosure. Privacy, on the other hand, encompasses the patient's right to control access to their personal health information and to maintain autonomy over its use.

- Confidentiality: Healthcare providers have a legal and ethical duty to maintain the confidentiality of patient information. This includes protecting both written and electronic records, as well as verbal communications, from unauthorized access or disclosure.

- Privacy: Patients have the right to privacy regarding their health information, including the right to control who has access to their medical records and how their information is used. Healthcare providers must respect patient privacy preferences and obtain consent before sharing information with third parties.

Ethical Considerations

Respecting confidentiality and privacy is not only a matter of legal compliance but also an ethical imperative that fosters trust and respect in the patient-provider relationship.

- Trust and Respect: Confidentiality and privacy are essential for building trust between patients and healthcare providers. Patients must feel confident that their personal health information will be kept confidential and that their privacy rights will be respected.
- Autonomy and Self-Determination: Respecting patient confidentiality and privacy upholds the principles of autonomy and self-determination. Patients have the right to control access to their health information and make decisions about how it is used.
- Beneficence and Non-Maleficence: Protecting patient confidentiality and privacy promotes beneficence by ensuring that patients receive care without fear of judgment or discrimination. It also upholds the principle of non-maleficence by preventing harm that could result from unauthorized disclosure of sensitive information.

Legal Requirements

In addition to ethical considerations, healthcare providers must adhere to legal requirements regarding confidentiality and privacy, including:

- Health Insurance Portability and Accountability Act (HIPAA): HIPAA is a federal law that establishes privacy and security standards for protecting patient health information.

Covered entities, including healthcare providers and health plans, must comply with HIPAA regulations to safeguard patient privacy and confidentiality.
- State Laws: Many states have additional laws and regulations governing the confidentiality and privacy of health information. Healthcare providers must be aware of and comply with these state-specific requirements in addition to HIPAA.

Safeguarding Patient Information

To protect patient confidentiality and privacy, respiratory therapists can implement various strategies:

- Secure Documentation: Ensure that patient records are stored securely, whether in electronic or paper format, to prevent unauthorized access or disclosure.
- Access Controls: Limit access to patient information to authorized individuals only and implement password protection and encryption measures to prevent data breaches.
- Verbal Communication: Exercise caution when discussing patient information in public areas to avoid inadvertent disclosure. Use private spaces or secure communication channels for sensitive discussions.
- Informed Consent: Obtain informed consent from patients before sharing their health information with third parties, except in cases where disclosure is required by law or necessary for patient care.

Challenges and Considerations

Maintaining confidentiality and privacy in respiratory care may present challenges, particularly in settings where multiple healthcare providers are involved in patient care or where electronic health records are used. To address these challenges, respiratory therapists can:

- Communicate Effectively: Foster open communication with patients about the importance of confidentiality and privacy and address any concerns they may have.
- Collaborate with Interdisciplinary Teams: Work collaboratively with other healthcare providers to ensure that patient information is shared securely and only when necessary for patient care.
- Stay Informed: Stay up to date on changes in privacy and security regulations, as well as best practices for protecting patient information in respiratory care settings.

Confidentiality and privacy are foundational principles in respiratory care that are essential for upholding ethical standards, fostering trust, and protecting patient rights. By respecting patient confidentiality, maintaining privacy safeguards, and complying with legal requirements, respiratory therapists can fulfill their ethical and professional responsibilities while providing high-quality care to their patients. Understanding the importance of confidentiality and privacy and implementing strategies to safeguard patient information are crucial steps in promoting patient-centered care and maintaining the integrity of the patient-provider relationship.

DISCUSSION QUESTIONS

- What steps can respiratory therapists take to ensure ethical decision-making in complex clinical situations?
- Discuss a hypothetical case where a respiratory therapist faces an ethical dilemma. What factors should be considered in making the final decision?

MODULE THREE

LESSON ONE: ETHICAL DILEMMAS AND DECISION-MAKING IN RESPIRATORY CARE

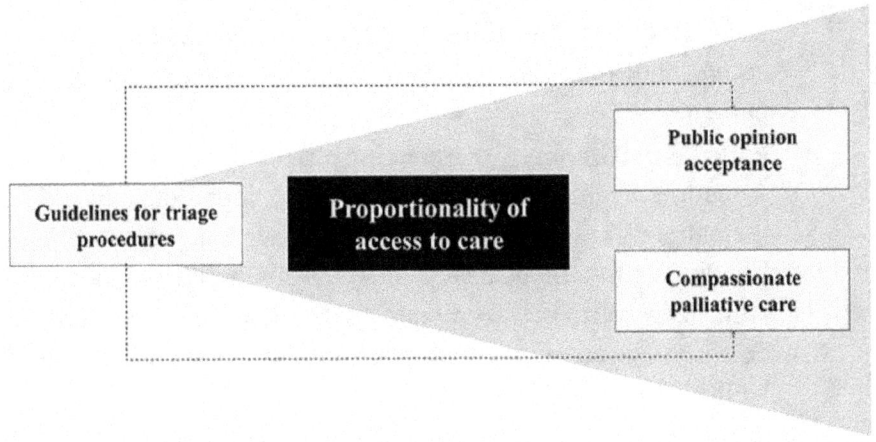

Ethical dilemmas are inherent in healthcare practice and can arise when there are conflicting values, principles, or interests at play. In respiratory care, where decisions often have life-altering consequences for patients, healthcare providers may encounter complex ethical challenges that require careful consideration and thoughtful decision-making. This lesson explores common ethical dilemmas in respiratory care, ethical frameworks for decision-making, and strategies for navigating these challenging situations.

Understanding Ethical Dilemmas

Ethical dilemmas occur when there are competing moral obligations or principles that make it difficult to determine the right course of action. In respiratory care, ethical dilemmas may arise in various contexts, including end-of-life care, resource allocation, and patient autonomy.

- End-of-Life Care: Decisions about withdrawing or withholding life-sustaining treatments, such as mechanical ventilation, can present ethical dilemmas for respiratory therapists. Balancing the principles of autonomy, beneficence, and non-maleficence while respecting patient wishes and values is essential in these situations.

- Resource Allocation: During times of scarcity, such as a pandemic or natural disaster, respiratory therapists may face ethical dilemmas related to the allocation of limited resources, such as ventilators. Ethical considerations include fairness, equity, and maximizing benefits for the greatest number of patients.
- Patient Autonomy: Respecting patient autonomy can sometimes conflict with healthcare providers' duty to act in the patient's best interest. For example, when a patient refuses life-saving treatment based on religious beliefs or personal values, respiratory therapists must navigate the tension between respecting the patient's autonomy and ensuring their well-being.

Ethical Frameworks for Decision-Making

Ethical frameworks provide a structured approach to analyzing and resolving ethical dilemmas. Several frameworks are commonly used in healthcare settings, including:

- Principlism: Principlism is based on four ethical principles: autonomy, beneficence, non-maleficence, and justice. This framework involves identifying the relevant principles in a given situation and weighing them to determine the most ethically justifiable course of action.
- Utilitarianism: Utilitarianism evaluates actions based on their consequences and seeks to maximize overall happiness or well-being. In respiratory care, this framework may involve choosing the course of action that produces the greatest benefit for the greatest number of patients.
- Virtue Ethics: Virtue ethics focuses on the character and moral virtues of the individual. Practitioners apply this framework by considering which actions align with virtuous traits such as compassion, integrity, and honesty.

Strategies for Navigating Ethical Dilemmas

Respiratory therapists can employ several strategies to navigate ethical dilemmas effectively:

- Ethics Consultation: Seeking input from ethics committees or consulting with ethicists can provide valuable insights and guidance when facing complex ethical dilemmas.
- Multidisciplinary Collaboration: Collaborating with other healthcare professionals, including physicians, nurses, social workers, and ethicists, can help generate diverse perspectives and identify creative solutions to ethical challenges.
- Reflective Practice: Engaging in reflective practice involves critically examining one's values, beliefs, and actions to identify underlying assumptions and biases. This self-reflection can enhance ethical awareness and decision-making skills.
- Advance Care Planning: Encouraging patients to engage in advance care planning discussions can help clarify their values, preferences, and goals of care, facilitating more informed decision-making in future healthcare decisions.

Case Studies

Examining real-world case studies can provide valuable insights into how ethical principles are applied in respiratory care practice. Here are two hypothetical case studies illustrating common ethical dilemmas:

Case Study 1: End-of-Life Decision: A patient with end-stage COPD is admitted to the hospital with respiratory failure. The patient's family insists on continuing aggressive treatments, despite the patient's expressed desire to forego life-sustaining interventions. The respiratory therapist must navigate the tension between respecting the patient's autonomy and honoring their wishes while providing compassionate care to both the patient and their family.

Case Study 2: Resource Allocation: During a severe flu outbreak, the hospital's ventilator supply becomes depleted, and multiple patients require mechanical ventilation. The respiratory therapist is tasked with triaging patients and determining who will receive access to ventilators. The therapist must consider ethical principles of fairness, equity, and maximizing benefits to make difficult decisions in a time of scarcity.

DISCUSSION QUESTIONS

- What are the essential elements of informed consent, and why are they particularly important in respiratory care?
- How should a respiratory therapist approach a situation where a patient refuses a recommended treatment?

LESSON TWO: PROFESSIONALISM AND ETHICAL PRACTICE IN RESPIRATORY CARE

Professionalism and ethical practice are integral components of providing high-quality care in respiratory therapy. As respiratory therapists, maintaining professionalism and adhering to ethical principles are essential for promoting patient safety, ensuring trust in the healthcare system, and upholding the integrity of the profession. This lesson explores the significance of professionalism and ethical practice in respiratory care, key principles of professional conduct, and strategies for fostering a culture of ethical excellence.

The Importance of Professionalism

Professionalism encompasses the attitudes, behaviors, and values that characterize competent and ethical practice in respiratory care. It involves demonstrating integrity, compassion, accountability, and respect for patients, colleagues, and the profession.

- Patient Safety: Professionalism is essential for ensuring patient safety and quality of care. Respiratory therapists must adhere to professional standards and best practices to minimize risks and prevent errors that could harm patients.
- Trust and Confidence: Professionalism builds trust and confidence in the healthcare system among patients, families, and the public. Patients rely on respiratory therapists to deliver competent and compassionate care, and professionalism is essential for maintaining their trust and confidence.
- Professional Growth: Professionalism involves a commitment to lifelong learning and continuous improvement. Respiratory therapists must stay abreast of advances in the field, engage in professional development activities, and adhere to ethical standards to enhance their skills and knowledge.

Ethical Principles in Professional Practice

Ethical practice in respiratory care is guided by several core principles that govern professional conduct and decision-making. These principles include:

- Integrity: Respiratory therapists must demonstrate honesty, transparency, and accountability in their interactions with patients, colleagues, and the public. Upholding integrity is essential for maintaining trust and credibility in the profession.
- Compassion: Compassion involves showing empathy, kindness, and sensitivity to the needs and feelings of patients and their families. Respiratory therapists must approach patient care with compassion and understanding, recognizing the unique challenges and vulnerabilities that patients may face.
- Respect: Respect for patient autonomy, dignity, and rights is fundamental to ethical practice. Respiratory therapists must treat patients with respect and dignity, regardless of their background, beliefs, or circumstances.

- Professional Boundaries: Maintaining appropriate professional boundaries is essential for ensuring ethical practice and protecting patients from harm. Respiratory therapists must establish clear boundaries in their relationships with patients and colleagues and avoid conflicts of interest or dual relationships that could compromise their integrity.

Strategies for Professionalism and Ethical Practice

Respiratory therapists can promote professionalism and ethical practice by:

- Adhering to Standards: Familiarize yourself with professional codes of ethics, practice guidelines, and regulatory requirements that govern respiratory care practice. Adhering to these standards ensures that you meet professional expectations and uphold ethical principles.
- Seeking Feedback: Solicit feedback from colleagues, supervisors, and patients to identify areas for improvement and ensure that your practice aligns with professional standards and ethical principles.
- Reflective Practice: Engage in reflective practice to critically evaluate your actions, decisions, and interactions with patients and colleagues. Reflective practice fosters self-awareness, enhances learning, and promotes professional growth.
- Continuous Learning: Stay informed about advances in respiratory care, evidence-based practices, and ethical considerations through ongoing education, professional development activities, and participation in professional organizations.

Ethical Challenges in Professional Practice

Respiratory therapists may encounter various ethical challenges in their professional practice, including:

- Conflicts of Interest: Balancing professional obligations with personal interests or external influences can present ethical

dilemmas. Respiratory therapists must prioritize patient welfare and avoid conflicts of interest that could compromise their objectivity or integrity.
- Informed Consent: Obtaining valid informed consent from patients can be challenging, particularly in complex or urgent situations. Respiratory therapists must ensure that patients understand their treatment options, risks, and benefits and have the capacity to make informed decisions.
- Cultural Competence: Providing culturally competent care requires sensitivity to patients' cultural beliefs, values, and preferences. Respiratory therapists must be aware of cultural differences and adapt their communication and care practices accordingly to ensure respect for patient diversity.

Professionalism and ethical practice are foundational principles in respiratory care that underpin the delivery of safe, compassionate, and patient-centered care. By upholding integrity, demonstrating compassion, respecting patient autonomy, and maintaining professional boundaries, respiratory therapists can promote trust, enhance patient safety, and contribute to the integrity and credibility of the profession. Ethical awareness, reflective practice, and ongoing professional development are essential for navigating ethical challenges, promoting professionalism, and ensuring ethical excellence in respiratory care practice.

DISCUSSION QUESTIONS

- How does professionalism in respiratory care influence patient outcomes and trust in the healthcare system?
- What are some strategies for respiratory therapists to maintain professionalism and ethical practice in their day-to-day work?

MODULE FOUR

LESSON ONE: LEGAL RESPONSIBILITIES AND RISK MANAGEMENT IN RESPIRATORY CARE

Patient-level factors (Practitioners' perspectives)
- Knowledge and understanding
- Motivation and taking responsibility
- Personal life circumstances/context
- Specific self-management skills
- Social/support network
- Emotional and psychological issues

Organisational/system-level factors
- Fragmentation of COPD services, interventions and resources
- Inconsistent COPD care and referral pathways.
- Focus on biomedical model and outcomes for COPD
- Communication and information-sharing infrastructure
- Organisation of care
- Normalizing self-management into routine practice.

Practitioner-level factors
- Practitioners' knowledge and understanding
- Consultation and communication skills
- Multidisciplinary team-working and communication
- Frustration/treatment futility
- Speciality, interest and expertise in COPD/respiratory conditions

Respiratory therapists have legal responsibilities to their patients, colleagues, employers, and the healthcare system as a whole. Understanding these legal obligations and taking proactive steps to manage risks are essential aspects of professional practice. This lesson explores the legal framework governing respiratory care, common legal issues encountered by respiratory therapists, and strategies for mitigating legal risks and ensuring compliance with legal requirements.

Legal Framework in Respiratory Care

The legal framework for respiratory care practice is multifaceted and encompasses various laws, regulations, and standards at the federal, state, and institutional levels.

- Federal Laws and Regulations: Federal laws such as the Health Insurance Portability and Accountability Act (HIPAA), the Emergency Medical Treatment and Labor Act (EMTALA), and the Americans with Disabilities Act (ADA) establish standards for patient privacy, emergency care, and accessibility, among other areas. Respiratory therapists must comply with these federal laws to ensure patient safety and protect their rights.
- State Laws and Regulations: Each state has its own set of laws and regulations governing the practice of respiratory care, including licensure requirements, scope of practice guidelines, and professional conduct standards. Respiratory therapists must be familiar with and adhere to the laws and regulations specific to their state of practice.
- Institutional Policies and Guidelines: Healthcare institutions may have their own policies, procedures, and guidelines that respiratory therapists must follow to ensure compliance with legal requirements and promote patient safety. These institutional policies may address areas such as documentation, informed consent, and professional conduct.

Common Legal Issues in Respiratory Care

Respiratory therapists may encounter various legal issues in their practice, including:

- Malpractice Claims: Allegations of negligence or malpractice can arise if a respiratory therapist fails to meet the standard of care, resulting in harm to a patient. Common issues that may lead to malpractice claims include medication errors, failure to monitor patients, and improper documentation.

- Documentation Errors: Inadequate or inaccurate documentation can lead to legal and regulatory issues, including allegations of negligence, billing fraud, and regulatory violations. Respiratory therapists must maintain detailed and accurate patient records to ensure continuity of care and legal compliance.
- Scope of Practice Violations: Performing procedures or interventions outside the scope of practice authorized by state law can result in disciplinary action, licensure revocation, or legal liability. Respiratory therapists must adhere to the scope of practice guidelines established by their state regulatory board and seek additional training or certification as necessary.

Strategies for Risk Management

To mitigate legal risks and ensure compliance with legal requirements, respiratory therapists can implement several strategies:

- Adherence to Standards of Care: Practice in accordance with professional standards of care and evidence-based guidelines to minimize the risk of adverse outcomes and legal liability.
- Documentation Practices: Maintain thorough and accurate documentation of patient assessments, interventions, and communications to support clinical decision-making, facilitate continuity of care, and demonstrate compliance with legal and regulatory requirements.
- Informed Consent: Obtain valid informed consent from patients or their authorized representatives before performing medical procedures or interventions, ensuring that patients understand the nature, risks, and benefits of the proposed treatment.
- Continuing Education and Training: Stay informed about changes in laws, regulations, and standards of practice through ongoing education, training, and professional development activities. This includes staying up to date on

advancements in respiratory care technology and evidence-based practices.
- Collaboration and Communication: Foster open communication and collaboration with interdisciplinary healthcare teams, patients, and their families to promote patient safety, enhance quality of care, and mitigate legal risks.

Legal and Ethical Decision-Making

Respiratory therapists must navigate legal and ethical considerations in their practice and make decisions that uphold patient welfare and promote professional integrity. When faced with complex legal or ethical dilemmas, respiratory therapists can consult with legal counsel, ethics committees, or professional organizations for guidance and support.

Legal responsibilities and risk management are integral aspects of professional practice in respiratory care. By understanding the legal framework governing their practice, identifying common legal issues, and implementing strategies for risk management and legal compliance, respiratory therapists can minimize legal risks, protect patient safety, and maintain the trust and confidence of their patients and colleagues. Ethical decision-making, effective communication, and ongoing professional development are essential for navigating legal challenges and promoting high-quality, ethical care in respiratory therapy practice.

DISCUSSION QUESTIONS

- What are some common legal issues that respiratory therapists might encounter, and how can they mitigate these risks?
- How can respiratory therapists balance their legal responsibilities with the ethical obligation to provide the best possible care to patients?

MODULE FIVE

LESSON ONE: PROFESSIONAL DEVELOPMENT AND ADVOCACY IN RESPIRATORY CARE

Professional development and advocacy play critical roles in advancing the field of respiratory care and promoting the interests of respiratory therapists, patients, and the broader healthcare community. We will explore the importance of ongoing professional development, strategies for advocating for the profession, and opportunities for engagement and leadership in respiratory care.

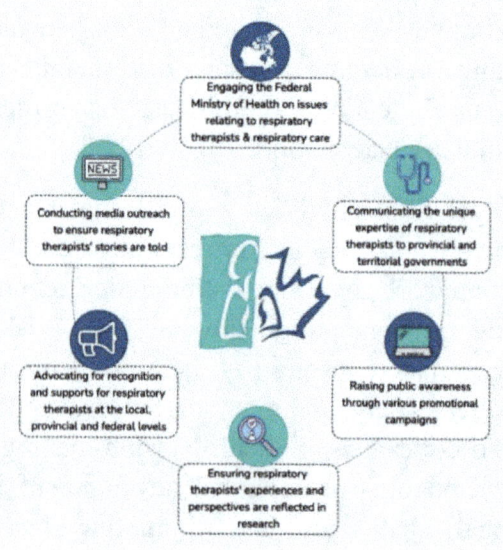

Importance of Professional Development

Professional development is essential for respiratory therapists to stay current with advancements in the field, enhance their clinical skills, and meet evolving healthcare needs. Continuous learning and skill development contribute to improved patient outcomes, career satisfaction, and professional growth.

- Continuing Education: Participate in continuing education activities, such as conferences, workshops, and online

courses, to expand your knowledge base, stay abreast of emerging trends, and enhance your clinical skills.
- Certification and Licensure: Pursue specialty certifications and maintain licensure requirements to demonstrate competency and commitment to professional excellence. Specialty certifications can provide opportunities for career advancement and specialization in areas of interest.
- Clinical Experience: Seek opportunities for hands-on clinical experience and exposure to diverse patient populations and practice settings to broaden your skills and knowledge as a respiratory therapist.

Advocacy for the Profession

Advocacy is essential for promoting the interests of respiratory therapists, advocating for patient rights, and influencing healthcare policy and legislation. Respiratory therapists can engage in advocacy at the local, state, and national levels to advance the profession and improve patient care.

- Legislative Advocacy: Advocate for legislation that supports the role of respiratory therapists, promotes patient safety, and addresses key issues affecting the profession, such as scope of practice, reimbursement, and healthcare reform.
- Public Awareness Campaigns: Raise awareness about the value of respiratory therapy and the vital role that respiratory therapists play in patient care through public education campaigns, community outreach initiatives, and media engagement.
- Professional Organizations: Join professional organizations such as the American Association for Respiratory Care (AARC) and participate in advocacy efforts, policy development, and grassroots initiatives to advance the profession and amplify the voice of respiratory therapists.

Opportunities for Engagement and Leadership

Engaging in leadership roles and professional organizations can provide opportunities for networking, mentorship, and career advancement in respiratory care.

- Leadership Development: Take on leadership roles within your healthcare organization, professional association, or community to develop leadership skills, foster collaboration, and drive positive change in respiratory care practice.
- Mentorship and Networking: Seek out mentorship opportunities and build professional networks with colleagues, mentors, and industry leaders to exchange knowledge, share best practices, and support career development.
- Research and Scholarship: Contribute to the advancement of respiratory care through research, scholarship, and publication of clinical findings and innovations. Participate in research projects, quality improvement initiatives, and evidence-based practice initiatives to improve patient outcomes and contribute to the body of knowledge in respiratory therapy.

DISCUSSION QUESTIONS

- Why is ongoing professional development important for respiratory therapists, and what are some effective ways to pursue it?
- How can respiratory therapists advocate for their profession and for the patients they serve?

MODULE SIX

LESSON ONE: ETHICAL LEADERSHIP AND PROFESSIONAL RESPONSIBILITY

Ethical leadership and professional responsibility are integral aspects of effective leadership in respiratory care. Respiratory therapists in leadership roles have a responsibility to uphold ethical standards, promote a culture of integrity and accountability, and advocate for the interests of patients, colleagues, and the profession. In this lesson, we will explore the principles of ethical leadership, strategies for fostering a culture of ethical excellence, and the importance of professional responsibility in respiratory care leadership.

Principles of Ethical Leadership

Ethical leadership is characterized by integrity, transparency, and a commitment to ethical principles and values. Ethical leaders in respiratory care:

- Lead by Example: Ethical leaders demonstrate integrity, honesty, and transparency in their actions and decisions, serving as role models for ethical behavior and professional conduct.
- Promote Ethical Awareness: Ethical leaders foster a culture of ethical awareness and accountability within their organizations by providing education and training on ethical principles and encouraging open dialogue about ethical dilemmas and concerns.
- Respect for Stakeholders: Ethical leaders value the perspectives and contributions of all stakeholders, including patients, employees, and the community, and strive to make decisions that are in the best interests of those they serve.

Strategies for Ethical Leadership

Respiratory therapists in leadership roles can promote ethical leadership by:

- Setting Clear Expectations: Establish clear expectations and standards of conduct for employees, emphasizing the importance of ethical behavior, integrity, and professionalism in all aspects of respiratory care practice.
- Creating a Supportive Environment: Create a supportive and inclusive work environment where employees feel comfortable raising ethical concerns, seeking guidance, and reporting unethical behavior without fear of reprisal or retaliation.
- Ethical Decision-Making: Encourage ethical decision-making by providing resources, tools, and support to help employees navigate ethical dilemmas and make decisions that align with organizational values and ethical principles.

- Leading with Integrity: Lead by example and demonstrate integrity, honesty, and accountability in all interactions and decisions. Uphold ethical standards and hold yourself and others accountable for ethical conduct and professional behavior.

Professional Responsibility in Leadership

Respiratory therapists in leadership roles have a professional responsibility to:

- Advocate for Patients: Advocate for the interests and well-being of patients by ensuring access to high-quality care, promoting patient safety, and addressing systemic issues that impact patient outcomes and experiences.
- Support Professional Development: Support the professional development and growth of respiratory therapy staff by providing opportunities for education, training, and career advancement, and fostering a culture of continuous learning and improvement.
- Promote Collaboration and Teamwork: Foster collaboration and teamwork among respiratory therapy staff and interdisciplinary healthcare teams to improve communication, coordination of care, and patient outcomes.

Ethical leadership and professional responsibility are essential for fostering a culture of integrity, accountability, and excellence in respiratory care leadership. By demonstrating ethical leadership qualities, promoting a supportive and inclusive work environment, and advocating for the interests of patients and the profession, respiratory therapists can inspire trust, enhance organizational effectiveness, and contribute to the overall success and sustainability of respiratory care services. Embracing ethical leadership principles and professional responsibilities not only strengthens the profession but also enhances the quality and safety of patient care in respiratory therapy practice.

DISCUSSION QUESTIONS
- What qualities define an ethical leader in respiratory care, and how can these qualities be cultivated?
- Discuss the role of ethical leadership in fostering a positive work environment and improving patient care outcomes.

MODULE SEVEN

LESSON ONE: THE FUTURE OF ETHICS AND LEGAL ISSUES IN RESPIRATORY CARE

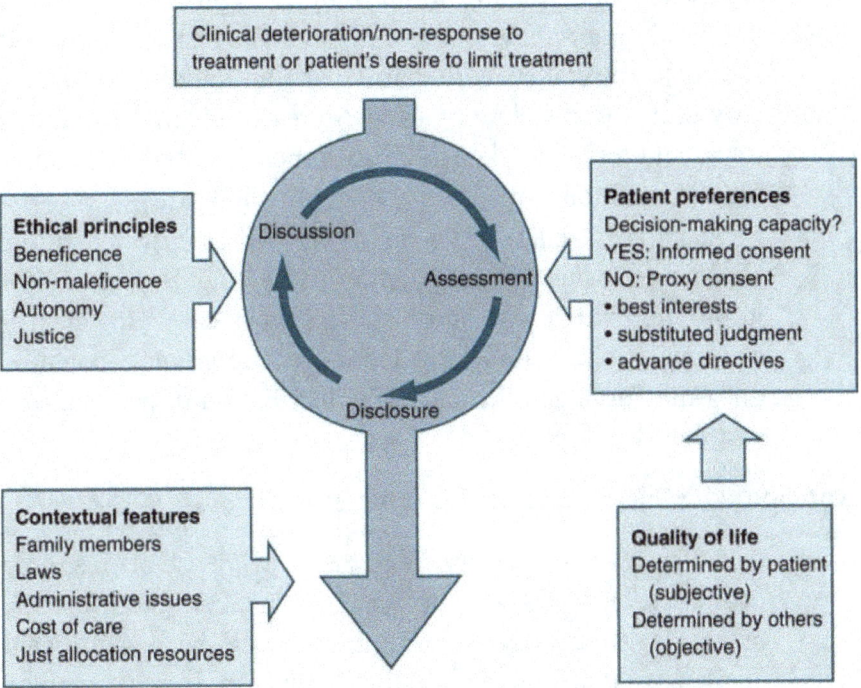

The field of respiratory care is continually evolving, influenced by advancements in medical technology, changes in healthcare policy, and shifts in societal expectations. As these changes unfold, new ethical and legal challenges will emerge, requiring respiratory therapists to remain vigilant, adaptable, and committed to ethical principles and legal compliance. This lesson explores the future of ethics and legal issues in respiratory care, focusing on emerging trends, anticipated challenges, and strategies for preparing for the future.

Emerging Trends in Respiratory Care

- Technological Advancements: Innovations in medical technology, such as telehealth, artificial intelligence (AI), and precision medicine, are transforming respiratory care. These advancements offer new opportunities for diagnosis, treatment, and patient monitoring but also raise ethical and legal questions regarding data privacy, informed consent, and equitable access to care.

- Telehealth and Remote Monitoring: The increasing use of telehealth and remote monitoring technologies has expanded access to respiratory care, particularly in underserved areas. However, these technologies also present challenges related to patient privacy, data security, and the need for robust regulatory frameworks to ensure quality and safety.
- Personalized Medicine: Personalized medicine, which tailors treatments to individual genetic profiles, holds promise for improving patient outcomes in respiratory care. However, it also raises ethical issues related to genetic privacy, potential discrimination, and the equitable distribution of personalized treatments.

Anticipated Ethical and Legal Challenges

- Data Privacy and Security: With the growing use of electronic health records (EHRs), telehealth, and AI, ensuring the privacy and security of patient data will be a significant challenge. Respiratory therapists must navigate complex regulations and implement robust security measures to protect patient information.
- Equity and Access: Ensuring equitable access to advanced respiratory care technologies and treatments will be critical. Ethical and legal frameworks must address disparities in healthcare access and outcomes, particularly for marginalized and vulnerable populations.
- Informed Consent in the Digital Age: As technology becomes more integrated into respiratory care, obtaining informed consent will become increasingly complex. Respiratory therapists must ensure that patients fully understand the implications of new technologies and treatments, including potential risks and benefits.

Strategies for Preparing for the Future

- Continuous Education and Training: Staying current with advancements in respiratory care and evolving ethical and legal standards is essential. Respiratory therapists should engage in lifelong learning through continuing education, professional development, and participation in professional organizations.
- Ethical and Legal Awareness: Developing a deep understanding of ethical principles and legal requirements in respiratory care is crucial. Respiratory therapists should stay informed about changes in laws, regulations, and ethical guidelines that impact their practice.
- Interdisciplinary Collaboration: Collaborating with other healthcare professionals, ethicists, and legal experts can help respiratory therapists navigate complex ethical and legal issues. Interdisciplinary teamwork promotes comprehensive and informed decision-making.
- Advocacy and Leadership: Taking an active role in advocacy and leadership can influence the future of respiratory care. Respiratory therapists should advocate for policies and practices that promote ethical excellence, patient safety, and equitable access to care.

DISCUSSION QUESTIONS

- How might advancements in technology impact the ethical and legal landscape of respiratory care in the future?
- What steps can respiratory therapists take to prepare for emerging ethical and legal challenges in their practice?

CONCLUSION

The intersection of ethics and legal issues in respiratory care is a critical area of focus for healthcare providers dedicated to delivering high-quality, patient-centered care. As respiratory therapists, understanding and navigating the complex ethical and legal landscapes of the profession is essential for ensuring patient safety, maintaining professional integrity, and fostering trust within the healthcare system.

The rapid advancements in medical technology, including telehealth and personalized medicine, bring new opportunities for improving patient outcomes but also introduce ethical and legal complexities that must be carefully navigated. Respiratory therapists must stay informed about these developments, engage in continuous professional development, and advocate for policies that promote equitable access to care and uphold the highest standards of practice.

The ethical and legal aspects of respiratory care are integral to the profession's foundation and future. By understanding and applying ethical principles, adhering to legal requirements, and advocating for professional development and patient rights, respiratory therapists can provide exceptional care that respects the dignity and diversity of all patients. This dedication to ethical and legal standards not only enhances the quality of care but also reinforces the trust and confidence placed in respiratory therapists by patients, colleagues, and the broader healthcare community.

REFERENCES

American Association for Respiratory Care (AARC). (2021). *AARC Clinical Practice Guidelines.* Dallas, TX: AARC.

Beauchamp, T. L., & Childress, J. F. (2019). *Principles of Biomedical Ethics.* Oxford University Press.

Buchbinder, S. B., & Shanks, N. H. (2016). *Introduction to Health Care Management.* Jones & Bartlett Learning.

Chochinov, H. M. (2007). *Dignity and the Essence of Medicine: The A, B, C, and D of Dignity Conserving Care.* BMJ.

Gawande, A. (2014). *Being Mortal: Medicine and What Matters in the End.* Metropolitan Books.

Giger, J. N. (2016). Transcultural Nursing: Assessment and Intervention (7th ed.). Elsevier.

Kohn, L. T., Corrigan, J. M., & Donaldson, M. S. (2000). *To Err Is Human: Building a Safer Health System.* National Academy Press.

Pope, T. M., & Anderson-Shaw, L. K. (2013*). Ethics in Healthcare: A Guide to Ethical Decision Making.* Springer Publishing Company.

Pozgar, G. D. (2019). *Legal and Ethical Issues for Health Professionals.* Jones & Bartlett Learning.

www.ingramcontent.com/pod-product-compliance
Lightning Source LLC
Chambersburg PA
CBHW050450010526
44118CB00013B/1762